THE
US ARMY
TODAY

THE US ARMY TODAY

DA LEVENSON

GALLERY BOOKS
An imprint of W.H. Smith Publishers Inc.
112 Madison Avenue
New York, New York 10016

A Bison Book

Published by Gallery Books
A Division of W H Smith Publishers Inc.
112 Madison Avenue
New York, New York 10016

Produced by
Bison Books Corp.
17 Sherwood Place
Greenwich, CT 06830

ISBN 8-8317-9075-X

Printed in Hong Kong

1 2 3 4 5 6 7 8 9 10

Picture Credits

All photos courtesy of the United States
Army except as noted below.
Bell Helicopter: 46 bottom.
Ford Aerospace & Communications
  Corporation: 40, 41, 48 both.
General Dynamics Land Systems: 24.
Sgt Dan Hardoby, US Army: 78 bottom,
  79 top.
LTV Aerospace and Defense Company,
  AM General Division: 37 top.
LTV Corporation: 50-51 all.
Richard Lee, courtesy of Office, Chief
  Army Reserve: 6, 23 top, 28-29, 32, 77
  top right, 81, 90-93 all.
McDonnell Douglas: 54-55.
Sikorsky Aircraft: 47 bottom, 52, 53
  second from top.
United States Air Force: 11 bottom,
  14, 15 all, 21, 22 bottom, 23 bottom,
  24-25, 39, 76, 77 top left, 96.
United States Department of Defense:
  2- 3, 7, 10 bottom, 12-13, 30 all, 36 top,
  37 bottom, 42-43, 44-45 all, 46 top, 47
  top, 57, 59 both, 70 top, 71 top, 78 top,
  79 middle right, 80, 82-83 all, 84-85 all,
  86-87, 88-89 all.

Acknowledgements

The author wishes to thank the following
people for supplying material to make
this book possible: Major Bruce Bell,
Office of the Chief of Public Affairs, US
Army; Bob Bockman and Ed Michalski,
Department of Defense; Bob DiMichele,
Training and Doctrine Command, US
Army; Frank Forestieri and Michael Ech-
ter, N W Ayer Incorporated; Sgt Dan Har-
doby, Recruiting Command, US Army;
Sheila Locke, Office of the Chief of Public
Affairs, US Army; and Connie Smith, Pub-
lic Affairs Office, Sixth US Army.

Edited by Carolyn Soto
Designed by Kathleen Jaeger

Page 1: Sunburned recruits march in
formation at Fort Campbell, Kentucky.

Page 2-3: Soldiers of the 82d Airborne
Division gather around the flag during a
pause in the action in Grenada in 1983.

Below: The Corps of Cadets assembled on
the Plain at the US Military Academy.

CONTENTS

INTRODUCTION TO THE UNITED STATES ARMY

In a complex and ever-changing world, the US Army is also changing. Today the Army is conducting the most extensive peacetime transition of its 200-year history. Integrated, forward-looking programs are underway, focused on improving organization and doctrine as well as equipping, manning and training troops. The goal: maximum power and the maximum use of that power.

Facing threats ranging from terrorist acts to strategic nuclear war, the Army must be flexible as well as strong. With an active troop force of 780,000 (compared to a Soviet army of three million), the US Army would be outnumbered in the event of a major-power conflict. Since the US forces will never equal those of their most dangerous potential foe, the decision was made in 1984 to maintain the present strength and concentrate on maximizing its use by reorganizing troops and modernizing weapons.

Opposite: **Infantrymen aim their M16s. The upgraded M16A2 is replacing the M16A1 as the Army's standard rifle.**

Right: **Recruits march and shout their 'jody calls' during basic training.**

A major obstacle to combat readiness is the extensive amounts of time and equipment it takes to deploy combat units overseas. To meet this challenge, the Army is restructuring combat divisions for more ready deployment and optimum use of weaponry. Light infantry divisions are being created — divisions with fewer troops and weapons that can be more rapidly deployed anywhere in the world. New weapons systems are modernizing the armor and mechanized divisions; these divisions are being restructured to accommodate systems such as the M1 Abrams tanks, the Bradley Fighting Vehicles and the Multiple Launch Rocket System. In addition, the Army is increasing its reliance on the reserve component forces — the Army Reserve and Army National Guard — and improving their equipment and combat readiness.

The basis for this comprehensive restructuring is the AirLand Battle Doctrine, the Army's blueprint for warfare that combines air and land power for maximum effectiveness. The spectrum of possible warfare runs from terrorism (the lowest level) to all-out nuclear war (highest level). Within the condi-

tion of nuclear stalemate, it is most likely that the US would become involved in a mid-level, or conventional, war if an armed conflict between major powers occurred. The AirLand Battle Doctrine provides a new, nonlinear approach to conventional warfare — one that would give 'leverage' to outnumbered US troops. New strategies, combat units and equipment are being developed to fight the increasing incidence of terrorism and low-intensity conflict.

As defense requirements change, so do training and recruiting requirements. Today, potential soldiers and officers must be better qualified than ever to gain admittance to the Army;

Opposite: **A camouflaged Ranger hones his skills during tactical exercise.**

Top: **Soldiers are briefed prior to 'battle' at the National Training Center.**

Below: **Soldiers depart an M2 Bradley Fighting Vehicle, operational since 1984.**

once in, they must continually improve to remain. Enhanced training and education programs ensure that the good get better. Combat training keeps pace with constantly evolving strategies and weapons systems, adding simulated combat exercises to standard field training.

Throughout this ambitious transition, the Army's 200-year-old mission remains the same — to deter aggression against the United States and her interests, and to fight and win if deterrence fails.

A BRIEF HISTORY

More than 200 years ago, the United States Army began as the Continental Army, formed by the Continental Congress on 14 June 1775 as a revolutionary force against England. Commanded by General George Washington, the new Army consisted of 10 rifle companies and the militias, which were volunteer,

part-time troops lent to Congress by the individual colonies. Many of the militiamen had fought in the French and Indian War of 1763, where they learned the guerilla-style battle techniques of the Indians. This was a prime factor in the Continental Army's victory over the British, who maintained their regimented, European combat style. More than 20,000 American soldiers served in the Revolutionary War.

Immediately following the Revolutionary War, only a few militia units remained intact to guard military supplies at West Point and Fort Pitt. Most of the regular troops were discharged, but the need for ready federal troops became obvious in 1785. The federal government had to borrow state troops to squelch the Whiskey Rebellion in western Pennsylvania and had to step in when state militias could not control Indian uprisings in Ohio, Indiana and Michigan. Congress established a new regular Army, an infantry regiment of 700, supplemented by state troops that came under federal control in wartime. In 1789 Congress established the War Department to direct military activity.

During the War of 1812, the regular Army, with a peak strength of 33,000

Left: **A soldier checks his parachute during airborne training. The three-week airborne course is a physical and mental challenge that prepares paratroopers for the ultimate — the jump** *(below).*

troops, was greatly outnumbered by the British. The states raised a temporary militia of 100,000 men, but most were poorly trained and many refused to cross the border into Canada in one of the major strategies of the war. However, the regular Army fought well and valiantly. Peace came when the British realized that in unsettled territory such as North America fighting could go on forever with neither side victorious. The postwar Army totaled 10,000 and was used to fight the Indians, who were revolting against the American takeover of their homelands. This Army fought two wars against the Seminole Indians in Florida and the Black Hawk Wars against the Sauk and Fox Indians in Illinois. The Army was also used to force the Cherokee to move to lands west of the Mississippi River, which at the time were considered undesirable by white settlers. The Regiment of Dragoons, forefather of today's 1st Cavalry, was formed in 1833, when the slow-moving infantry proved to be no match for the swift Indian warriors on horseback.

The borders of the young nation were pushed to the Pacific during the Mexican War (1846-48), when steam vessels were used to transport troops

Right and below: **Tank crew members from the 2d Infantry Division during 'Team Spirit 84'; and Army and Air Force personnel working shoulder-to-shoulder during 'Reforger 84' exercises in Europe.**

Army troops convene during a break in the action of 'Reforger' exercises in Germany. NATO conducts annual exercises in areas of Europe most likely to be strategic in the event of a conflict with Warsaw Pact nations.

beyond the US frontier. The regular Army was expanded to a peak strength of 115,000 during the war, but most regiments were disbanded after peace was established, and the Union Army entered the Civil War in 1861 with a mere 16,000 men. However, the Enrollment Act of 1863 instituted the draft, and the Union Army eventually reached a total strength of nearly one million.

The use of railroads, steam engines, and the telegraph, along with the improved range and accuracy of firearms, were major factors in the outcome of the Civil War. Soldiers fought in the unconventional, loose format acquired from the Indians but now strengthened by precision arms and improved transportation and communications systems. The nonindustrialized South was at a serious disadvantage and had tremendous difficulties arming, clothing and feeding its men. The Confederate Army, established by the Confederate Provisional Congress in 1861, reached a peak strength of 900,000 but casualties, disease, capture and desertion left only 174,223 to surrender in 1865.

Relentless war with the Indians throughout America continued until the remaining tribes just ceased to fight. The major campaigns were the Sioux Wars (1854-1890) in the northern plains (where Lieutenant Colonel George Custer made his legendary last stand against Sitting Bull) and the Apache Wars (1861-1900) in the Southwest.

In 1898, the United States Army entered the Spanish-American War with a small force of 28,000, which was doubled during the war and aided by 100,000 National Guardsmen and 125,000 volunteers. The Army was unorganized and ill prepared for battle under the tropical conditions found in Cuba and the Philippine Islands. As a result, a postwar reorganization took place in the early 1900s. The general staff system was established, as was the position of chief of staff.

With World War I came changes in

Both pages: Scenes from 'Reforger 84,' a NATO exercise held in Europe. A CH-53 helicopter from Semback Air Base, Germany (opposite); USAF C-130, carrying Army troops, is marshaled into the parking area at RAF Wildenroth, Germany (top); the 3/70 Armor, 5th Infantry Division, roll out of Coleman Barracks near Mannheim, Germany (middle); and Army equipment stored at Rhine Ordnance Depot (bottom).

Above: **The CH-47 medium-lift (bottom) and the XCH-62 heavy-lift helicopters.**

Opposite: **A recruit takes a break during basic training. Women, although excluded from combat, receive M16 rifle training.**

artillery and tactics. Airplanes and antiaircraft guns were in use, as were gas and chemical projectiles. New tactics included barrage fire, destructive fire to destroy trenches and neutralization fire to prevent enemy action. The regular Army increased to a peak of four million, but quick expansion caused confusion and inefficiency. After the war, the army was restructured: troops were reduced to about 200,000, while the number of officers was increased and used to train the National Guard and reserves. For the first time, emphasis was placed on theoretical study.

Further technological developments brought changes in the nature of warfare during World War II. Increased firepower and mechanization reduced the need for soldiers on the battlefield. Only 30 percent of the air and ground strength was in combat units; support

personnel made up the remaining 70 percent. Women entered the Army as nurses and later as members of the Women's Army Corps (WAC), filling staff and technical jobs as noncombatants, releasing more than 350,000 men for combat-related assignments overseas. The Selective Service Act of 1940 helped the Army reach its peak strength of 11 million during the war, reduced to 571,000 after peace was restored. The draft was discontinued in 1949, but quickly reinstated in 1950 following the outbreak of the Korean War.

The US had severely reduced troop strength just prior to a plea for assistance from the United Nations. As part of the UN international force in Korea, the Army gained experience in antiguerilla warfare. The Army grew to 1,596,000 by 1952, but totaled less than 1 million by 1957.

In the 1950s and early 1960s, the threat of atomic and then nuclear war prompted the restructuring of combat divisions into more mobile and flexible combat forces for use in smaller scale conventional battle. The US entered

into the North Atlantic Treaty Organization (NATO) to ensure the postwar defense of Europe.

As a member of the Southeast Asia Treaty Organization (SEATO), the US agreed to help check the spread of communism in Southeastern Asia and became involved in the Vietnam conflict in the late 1950s. Army troop strength in Vietnam grew from a small group of special advisers to a peak of 365,000 in 1969. In December 1972, 23,000 remained, and in 1973 all ground troops were removed. During the war, the airmobile division was first put into service, using helicopters and airplanes to support ground combat units. The helicopter emerged as one of the most vital pieces of machinery used by the Army. It performed scout and attack missions as well as transported cargo and troops. Its speed and efficiency as an ambulance helped keep the mortality rate of American wounded at less than one percent.

In 1973, the draft was abolished and a major reorganization began. The WAC was eliminated in 1978 and

Fresh-faced Army recruits during basic training. The quality of recruits has improved dramatically in the last decade, contributing to the overall strength of the current Army.

women were integrated into the mainstream. The Training and Doctrine Command (TRADOC) was established with the mission to determine and implement the doctrine and organization of the Army. TRADOC began plans for a smaller, lighter, more mobile force for use in conventional warfare, which evolved into the Army's current modernization programs.

A PERSONNEL PROFILE

Two hundred years ago, a man could join the Army if he 'could bring his own musket and uniform, did not have sore legs, scurvy, scale head, ruptures or other infirmities, and was able to carry his own weapon.' Today the Army's requirements are a bit more stringent. In fact it is so selective that 50 percent of those who apply are not accepted.

With worldwide commitments and the lowest peacetime personnel level in 30 years, the Army needs only high-quality people who can keep a smaller Army strong. The Army's 8800 recruiters actively pursue intelligent, motivated men and women to fill these needs.

Today's soldier is better educated than ever before. The percent of recruits with high school educations has increased from 54 percent in 1980 to 90 percent in 1984, and entrance exam scores have increased steadily as well. The minimum goal for all officers is a bachelor's degree. The Army has an 'up or out' policy, implemented with yearly testing and evaluation, that weeds out the soldier who does not improve physically and mentally and continue to be promoted.

A breakdown of manpower data shows that of the 780,000 active duty personnel, more than 107,000 are officers and 671,000 are enlisted; 214,000 are black, 28,000 are Hispanic, and 28,000 are other ethnic minorities. Of the 80,000 women in Army uniform, 10,000 are officers. The Army Reserve constitutes another 96,000 officers and 440,000 enlisted, while the Army National Guard has 42,000 officers and 401,000 enlisted personnel. In addition, the Army employs 450,000 civilians in positions ranging from administrators to foundry workers and scientists.

As its people continue to improve, so does the Army; its people are the Army's most vital source of power.

ORGANIZATION AND STRUCTURE

The United States Army is operated by the Department of the Army, one of the three military departments within the Department of Defense. The secretary of the Army is a civilian, appointed by the president and approved by the Senate. As head of the Department of the Army, he is accountable to the president through the secretary of Defense. The secretary of the Army conducts all affairs of the department, including its organization, administration and operation. The principal assistants to the secretary of the Army include the under secretary of the Army and various assistant secretaries, counsels and chiefs.

The Army Staff is the military staff of the secretary of the Army. Presided over by the chief of staff, it gives professional advice and assistance to the secretary of the Army and his assistants. It is responsible for the recruiting, supplying, equipping, organizing, training, mobilizing and demobilizing of the Army.

The chief of staff is the chief military adviser to the secretary of the Army and is responsible for the planning, development, execution, review and

Above: **Army troops disembark from an Air Force aircraft in Germany to participate in 'Reforger' readiness exercises.**

Opposite: **Light infantry divisions provide the Army with more flexible forces.**

analysis of the Army programs. He is the highest-ranking officer on active duty in the Army. He also presides over the Army general staff and the special staff.

The US Army consists of its headquarters — located in Washington, DC and containing the office of the secretary of the Army and the Army Staff — and the Army commands.

THE MAJOR ARMY COMMANDS

The US Army Forces Command (FORSCOM) is the largest of the Army's major commands. From its headquarters at Fort McPherson, Georgia, FORSCOM directs active Army and Army Reserve troops in every state but Hawaii, as well as in the Commonwealth of Puerto Rico and in the Virgin Islands of the United States. During a full mobilization, its total strength, including National Guard troops, would be more than 950,000, nearly two-thirds of the Army's total ground forces.

The commanding general of FORSCOM is responsible for the five continental US Armies (CONUSAs),

Above: **US Army Reserve soldiers on maneuvers. The Army is increasing its reliance on well-trained reserve troops.**

Below: **A member of the 9th Infantry Division during exercise 'Border Star 85.'**

the Third Army, all assigned FORSCOM active Army units and Army Reserve units. The commanders of the five continental Armies command the US Army Reserve and supervise the training of the National Guard within their area of supervision.

The five Continental Army areas are:
• First Army: headquarters Fort George G Meade, Maryland, responsible for the northeastern United States
• Second Army: headquarters Fort Gillem, Georgia, responsible for the southeastern United States, the Commonwealth of Puerto Rico and the Virgin Islands
• Fourth Army: headquarters Fort Sheridan, Illinois, responsible for the north-central United States
• Fifth Army: headquarters Fort Sam Houston, Texas, responsible for the south-central United States
• Sixth Army: headquarters Presidio of San Francisco, California, responsible for the western United States

Third Army, headquartered in Fort McPherson, Georgia, was reactivated in December 1982. It is unlike any other Army in Forces Command; its

mission is to quickly respond to situations threatening to US interests in Southwest Asia. Though part of FORSCOM, the headquarters Third Army is under the operational control of US Central Command (CENTCOM); if deployed, Third Army will be commanded by CENTCOM. Instead of a fixed structure of assigned units, Third Army selects specific forces to fill its current needs. Among those forces available to Third Army are the 82nd Airborne Division, the 101st Airborne Division, the 24th Infantry Division (Mechanized), the 6th Cavalry Brigade, Ranger and Special Forces units and many Reserve Component units.

The US Army, Europe (USAREUR), headquartered in Heidelberg, Germany, commands the Seventh Army (the Army's largest overseas combat unit), the US Army Southern European Task Force in Italy and Army forces in West Berlin. The United States, as a member of NATO, maintains the more than 200,000 Army personnel assigned to USAREUR in a constant state of readiness to deter armed aggression by Warsaw Pact forces. In the event of war, USAREUR would

transfer control of its combat forces to NATO's Central Army Group (CENTAG) while continuing to provide administrative and logistic support to its forces.

Eighth US Army is headquartered in Seoul, Korea. Along with other US armed services, it helps the Republic of Korea (ROK) to deter outside aggression in accordance with treaties between the US and the ROK. During wartime, Eighth Army would receive and ready forces for combat under the ROK-US Combined Forces Command.

US Army, Japan, headquartered in Zama, Japan, has about 2500 personnel who perform support and logistical operations for the Army in Japan and the western Pacific.

Western Command, (WESTCOM), headquarted at Fort Shafter, Hawaii, directs the 20,000 Army personnel in Hawaii. It is part of the US Pacific Command, which oversees American forces in Hawaii and the eastern Pacific.

Training and Doctrine Command (TRADOC) is responsible for the training of regular and reserve soldiers in preparation for war. TRADOC determines how the Army will fight, how it will be equipped and how it will be

organized. Its headquarters are at Fort Monroe, Virginia.

Army Materiel Command (AMC) is headquartered in Alexandria, Virginia. It has the mammoth task of developing, providing and maintaining weapons, equipment and supplies to the Army and its commands. It has the largest budget of all Army commands.

Information Systems Command plans, installs, engineers, operates and maintains assigned Army communications, base communications and Army air traffic control facilities as well as the Army portion of the Defense Communication System. Its headquarters are at Fort Huachuca, Arizona.

Intelligence and Security Command, one of the smallest commands, has a worldwide structure. From its Arlington Hall Station, Virginia headquarters, it directs intelligence collecting, counterintelligence, production and security operations.

Health Services Command provides health services for the Army within the United States, and for other governmental agencies and activities as directed. Its headquarters are at Fort Sam Houston, Texas.

Above and below: **The Army maintains its flexibility with numerous training and readiness exercises, including simulated combat maneuvers *(above)*, and large-scale joint-forces exercises such as 'Team Spirit,' held annually in Korea.**

Criminal Investigation Command, with headquarters in Washington, DC, conducts all Army major investigations, operates the Army's crime labs and provides personal security for Department of Defense and Department of the Army personnel.

Military Traffic Management Command (MTMC) directs the moving and storage of household goods of military personnel and manages military traffic, land transportation and common-user ocean terminal service within the continental United States. Its headquarters are in Washington, DC.

US Army Military District of Washington (USAMDW) provides base operation and support to the Army, Department of Defense and other government activities while defending assigned Department of Defense facilities.

US Army Corps of Engineers (USACE) directs the engineering, construction, operation and maintenance of Army and Air Force facilities worldwide. USACE develops, manages and executes the Army's Civil Works Programs, which involve engineering and real estate activities related to rivers, harbors and waterways. It protects and preserves navigable waters and assists in recovery from natural disasters.

THE ORGANIZATION OF COMBAT FORCES

The active Army force is made up of 17 combat divisions. Five are forward deployed, or most ready for combat; four of these are directed by US Army, Europe. and one is part of Eighth Army in South Korea. Eleven are stationed in the continental United States under Forces Command and one is based in Hawaii under the Western Command.

The division is the basic combined-arms unit. Under one command and

Below: **An on-line M1 Abrams prepares to attack simulated enemy positions during training exercises at Fort Bragg.**

Opposite: **A tank crew member during 'Border Star 85' exercises in Texas.**

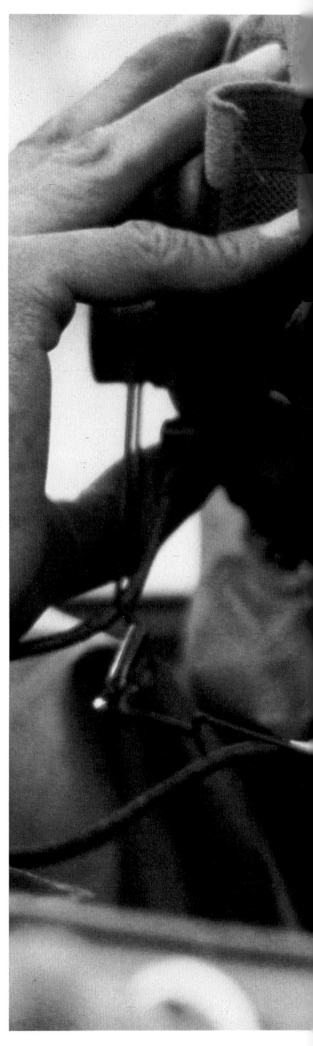

STERLING WHITE CORP.   PHILA, PA, 19132

MEAL, COMBAT, INDIVIDUAL
BEEF W/SPICED SAUCE,
B-1 UNIT

led by a major general, it is self-sufficient, containing support elements such as artillery, air defense artillery, intelligence, signal, chemical and engineer corps. Since it also includes combat service support elements such as transportation and medical services, it can function independently. However, for tactical reasons, two to five divisions often fight as part of a corps, which is commanded by a lieutenant general.

Each division contains six brigade-sized units, which are led by colonels. Each brigade is in turn made up of three to five battalions, the battalion being the basic maneuver unit, commanded by a lieutenent colonel and containing two or more companies of 150. Companies are led by captains and consist of two or more platoons of 40 men commanded by a lieutenant. Four squads (led by sergeants), the smallest combat units, make up a platoon. The number and types of battalions assigned by the command de-

Opposite: **One soldier seems pleased with his C-rations, the other not so sure.**

Below and overleaf: **Recruits in formation; and a soldier applies his buddy's camouflage make up.**

pend on force requirements determined by the the mission, the enemy and the terrain.

Light maneuver forces (light infantry, air assault infantry, airborne infantry and ranger infantry) are suited to close-in fighting in restricted terrain. Armor and mechanized forces maneuver well in open terrain, but are difficult to deploy and need considerable support once in the battlefield.

The Army does not have the airlift and sealift capability to deploy the most powerful and heavy equipment quickly in time of war, so it is restructuring light forces in order to meet its goal of greater strategic mobility. Light infantry divisions of 10,000 troops with fewer heavy weapons have been created that can deploy more quickly than the standard divisions of 16,000 men. A light infantry division can now be moved in 500 Air Force C-141 transports, compared to the more than 1000 it took to move a standard infantry division. Light divisions can be used as the primary force in low-intensity conflict, particularly in less developed areas of the world where no heavy forces are maintained. They can be followed by heavier forces if necessary and if the terrain warrants. They

would also be effective in mid- to high-intensity warfare as part of a corps force.

Armored and mechanized divisions are being redesigned for optimum use of new weapons and equipment, such as the Abrams M1 tank and the Bradley Fighting Vehicles, as well as for more rapid deployment. Troops are being cut from 19,000 to approximately 16,500. The modernization of heavy divisions is expected to continue into the 1990s as new weapons systems are fielded.

INFANTRY

The infantry, the largest combat arm, is the branch of the Army trained and equipped to fight on foot. Whether infantrymen march to battle, arrive by parachute, helicopter or ground vehicle, they attack and defend their position chiefly on foot.

There are two types of infantry divisions: light infantry, which is non-armored, and mechanized infantry, which travels in armored fighting vehicles.

Light divisions are a result of the Army's recent restructuring to deploy strategic forces more rapidly. They are

the smallest of all divisions, with an approximate strength of 10,000. A light infantry battalion contains about 380 men, structured in three infantry companies, one support company and a headquarters company.

Each solider carries his M16A2 rifle, which has replaced the automatic M16A1 as the Army's standard rifle. The M16A2 is lighter and can be fired in either a semiautomatic or three-burst automatic mode. In addition, easily portable weapons such as the MK19-3 grenade launcher, the M249 squad automatic weapon and the Dragon antitank missile are used by infantrymen. The Dragon is used in fewer numbers by light infantrymen as the emphasis now is on traveling 'light.'

Air assault infantry is a highly specialized force transported by helicopter, often past enemy ground defenses for the purpose of surprise attacks.

Airborne soldiers — paratroopers — are an elite group in the infantry. They are considered a strategic re-

This page: **A US-Honduran air-drop exercise in Honduras. Honduran troops prepare to board C-130 transports** *(top)*; **during the drop** *(middle)*; **and a paratrooper awaits his jump** *(bottom)*. **The Army conducts a variety of exercises in Honduras.**

serve, since they deploy to critical areas quickly.

Mechanized infantry has high mobility and armor protection, and can fight — mounted or dismounted — as part of a combined arms force. Mechanized infantry divisions contain about 15,800 men. Each battalion has around 890 men, a headquarters and headquarters company, three tank companies and a support company. Some mechanized divisions are being restructured under the Division 86 system for easier deployment and have fewer troops.

The Bradley Infantry Fighting Vehicle (IFV) affords armored antitank protection to mounted infantrymen while keeping pace with mobile armor forces. Dismounted, infantrymen can provide close-in protection for tanks in restricted areas.

Infantry training is conducted at the US Army Infantry School at Fort Benning, Georgia, which has been 'home of the Infantry' since 1918. Future infantrymen are trained in the use of

This page: **US Army Rangers during training exercises. Ranger training is often conducted under physical and mental conditions more severe than actual combat in order to produce highly skilled and confident leaders.**

weapons and mines; armored carrier operations; individual and squad tactical maneuvers; patroling; first aid; map reading; communications; and nuclear, biological and chemical defense.

Airborne training is also conducted at Fort Benning. Paratroopers go through a demanding three-week course that prepares them for jumping into a battle zone, ready to fight.

Rangers are a unique class of infantrymen. They are specially trained to conduct decentralized, independent operations anywhere in the world and are transported to their destination via land, sea or air. Their presence is sometimes used to demonstrate US resolve. They can conduct reconnaissance missions and raids deep in enemy territory, arriving by parachute, small boat, Navy vessel or on foot. The US Army Ranger Department is located at Fort Benning. Selected volunteers are trained there and on four other bases that provide wooded,

This page: **Scenes from the National Training Center, where 'opposing forces' are outfitted and equipped as Soviets.**

Opposite: **Exercises often include simulated chemical defense training.**

mountain, desert and jungle/swamp environments. For 58 days and nights, they undergo demanding training under extreme mental and physical stress to prepare them for the cutting edge of battle.

The first Ranger unit, Roger's Rangers, was formed in New Hampshire in 1756 to fight with the British in the French and Indian War. Since then, units have been formed as needed by the Army. The number of Rangers assigned to Ranger units was increased in 1984 to 2300. In 1983, US Army Rangers performed bravely and effi-

ciently during Operation Urgent Fury in Grenada.

ARMOR

The armor branch is the Army's mounted combat arm and consists of the armor and armored cavalry units. The armored cavalry is the direct successor to the horse cavalry and performs many of its traditional duties, including security, ground reconnaissance and active combat. Cavalry units can force an enemy into terrain where the main armor units can attack. The

Above and opposite above: **Two Army helicopters: the AH-64 Apache, a powerful and agile antitank weapon; and the UH-60 Black Hawk utility helicopter, which has the principal mission of troop deployment and resupply.**

Officers and enlisted soldiers are trained for mounted combat at the Armor Center at Fort Knox, Kentucky. Hands-on training is emphasized and new techniques including laser firing are employed. Officers receive training in all crew duties before moving on to tactical exercises.

AVIATION

Army aircraft play a vital part in modern warfare, as they fill combat, reconnaissance and transport roles. Attack helicopters, such as the AH-64 Apache, provide excellent strike and maneuver power, particularly when they work in conjunction with ground armor and cavalry units. Scout helicopters spot enemy positions and take aerial photographs. Small surveillance airplanes provide intelligence and communication to combat units. Utility helicopters, such

Bradley Cavalry Fighting Vehicle (CFV) is used for security and reconnaissance missions. It is replacing the M113A2 Armored Personnel Carrier as the primary vehicle for the armored cavalry. The size and configuration of cavalry units vary considerably. A cavalry squadron may or may not contain tanks and/or helicopters. Brigade-sized cavalry units are still referred to as 'regiments,' a throwback to the days when regiments of Army soldiers swept across the plains of the western

frontier on horseback.

'Armor' means tanks. An armored battalion contains approximately 50 tanks, 550 officers and men, with a headquarters, headquarters company, three tank companies and a combat support company. Offensively, the M1 Abrams and the M60 tanks are used to penetrate the enemy's defenses or to outflank its forces. They are also used for rapid pursuit. Defensively, they maneuver rapidly to increase firepower where necessary.

Right and opposite: **Aircraft employed in combined arms combat training at the Army's National Training Center. The Air Force A-10 'Warthog'** *(opposite)* **provides close air support to ground troops, as does the AH-64 Apache attack helicopter.**

as the UH-60A Black Hawk, are transportation vehicles. They move troops and equipment in and out of battle areas quickly. They are also used as ambulances. About 2000 personnel (10 percent women) are trained at Fort Rucker, Alabama in aviation-related occupational specialties, including mechanics, air traffic control and flight operations. To win his wings, an Army pilot must complete flight school at Fort Rucker, one of the most demanding training programs the Army offers.

FIELD ARTILLERY

The field artillery unit uses firepower to support the other combat arms, especially infantry, on the battlefield. It can neutralize enemy firepower and protect soldiers in a defensive position. Artillery units contain about 2300 troops and a

group of nuclear and nonnuclear weapons, including the howitzer canons, the Multiple Launch Rocket System (MLRS) and the Firefinder weapon-detection system. Artillery is transported by various means, from heavy trucks to utility helicopters such as the new UH-60A Black Hawk and the CH-47 Chinook. The Field Artillery Training Center at Fort Sill, Oklahoma annually trains 26,000 recruits in artillery-related occupational specialties.

AIR DEFENSE ARTILLERY

Air defense artillery units defend all ground forces against attack by enemy aircraft. To accomplish this mission, they employ several surface-to-air missile systems, including the shoulder-fired Stinger, the Chaparral, the Hawk and the Patriot.

Air defense training is conducted at Fort Bliss, Texas. About 8000 soldiers are trained there each year, a small percent of whom are women trained in support services.

COMBAT ENGINEERS

Engineer units play an important combat role. They provide essential construction to combat forces in the field. Often working under fire, they construct landing strips, bridges, roads and fortifications; they also emplace mine fields and obstacles. Engineering equipment, such as cranes, tractors and dump trucks, is often delivered to the unit by aircraft and is sometimes para-

Opposite page: **Army engineer training. National Guard combat engineers during road-building exercises in Panama** *(top);* **and** *(bottom)* **a welder at work. Welding is one of the many engineer occupational roles.**

Above: **The HUMMER (high-mobility, multi-purpose wheeled vehicle), a recently fielded one-and-a-quarter-ton truck.**

Below: **Combat engineers at work during training exercises in Panama.**

Above and below: Special Forces personnel in training exercises. Special Forces training is the most grueling of any in the Army and includes demolition work *(above)*, as well as many arduous weeks spent in various terrains in preparation for their unconventional, independent style of warfare.

chuted in. In addition, units have floating bridges, inflatable assault boats and rafts.

Over 40,000 personnel are trained annually at Fort Leonard Wood, Missouri in various combat engineer occupational roles, such as engineers, plumbers, electricians, construction workers and vehicle operators and mechanics.

SPECIAL FORCES

The members of the Special Forces are better known as 'Green Berets' for their distinctive hats that set them apart from the Army at large. This elite group of rigorously trained men go where general purpose force cannot go. They conduct unconventional warfare in specially trained and organized units capable of independent operations. They are assigned to overt, covert or clandestine operations, in peace or war, that complement general purpose forces' capabilities. Their missions may involve strategic intelligence, psychological operations, Ranger operations, strike operations and related special operations. The First Special Service Force was formed in 1942, but the Special Forces lineage can be traced back to Rogers' Rangers, the first Ranger unit in America, which was formed 20 years prior to the Revolutionary War. The US Army Special Forces was established in 1952; many of its initial members were former Rangers who wanted further training in the unconventional type of warfare they had successfully used during World War II and the Korean War. They were looking for excitement, and they found it.

Special Forces training is the most extensive and the most demanding, physically and mentally, of any in the Army. After meeting stringent requirements including secret security clearance, soldiers spend from 24 to 58 weeks or longer training in swamp, jungle, amphibious, desert and arctic environments. Their preparation includes training in foreign languages and weapons, medical treatment and demolition.

Special Forces are also used in the area of foreign internal defense and nation building. As advisory groups, they help nations to build and train their armed forces.

Opposite: A member of the 1st Special Forces prepares to make a jump during 'Team Spirit' in Korea.

WEAPONS OF THE UNITED STATES ARMY

Today the Army is in the early stages of its weapons-modernization program. The present restructuring is expected to continue into the 1990s; the Army plans to field 400 new systems in the next 10 years. Following is a selection of some of the Army's key weapons systems currently in the field, categorized by the type of combat in which they are used.

CLOSE COMBAT WEAPONRY

Close combat involves the use of direct combat power at close range — weapon to weapon, man to man. The weapons employed in this type of fighting include tanks used by armored battalions; fighting vehicle systems and armored personnel carriers used by mechanized infantry; direct line-of-sight weapons and short-range mortars used by infantrymen.

The M1 Abrams tank is the Army's primary ground combat weapon system for closing with and destroying enemy forces by employing shock action, mobility and firepower. The M1 is used in conjunction with other ground and air systems under all battlefield conditions. The Abrams has special armor and a fire-detection and suppression system. Fuel and ammunition are stored away from the

Both pages: **The Night Chaparral, the type of Chaparral short-range, air defense system capable of night operations. In central Europe, Night Chaparral could operate 85% of the time.**

four-man crew. These factors make it less vulnerable and more survivable than its predecessors such as the M60 series. Its shoot-on-the-move capability and improved day-night fire control insure that it delivers accurate and lethal fire on both armored and unprotected targets. The 1500 hp turbine engine and improved suspension allow the 60-ton tank to move quickly across the battlefield at a top speed of 30 mph (top road speed, 45 mph), reducing the tank's exposure to enemy weapons.

The engine's high fuel consumption (a reported 1.9 mpg when first fielded in 1982) has been a target for the critics of the M1 program. However, the Army contends that the M1 is capable of operating through a 24-hour combat day without refueling. The tank has met the 275-mile-range requirements at 30 mph. The M1 uses about 32 percent more fuel, requiring more support vehicles, than the M60 series tanks, while its engine power is roughly 100 percent greater. The main gun of the M1 is the M68E1 105mm rifled gun, the standard main armament on US and most NATO tanks. The first production model of the improved M1, the M1E1, was produced in 1985 and features a 120mm smooth-bore gun and NBC overpressure protective system. It weighs three tons

more than the M1 and is capable of a top road speed of 41.5 mph. In addition, the Army is pursuing a product improvement program to maintain the Abrams' competitive position through the 1980s and beyond.

The M60A3 is an improved version of the Army's M60 series tank, which has been in the field since 1961 and was the Army's main battle tank before the M1 was deployed. First-round hit capability has been enhanced for the

Previous page: **The M1 Abrams main battle tank** *(left)* **and the Bradley Fighting Vehicle. Mechanized divisions are being restructured to accommodate them.**

A3 by means of stabilization and the inclusion of a rangefinder, solid-state computer and thermal shroud. Fighting capability during periods of reduced visibility has been improved with the addition of the tank thermal imaging sight. M60A1 tanks are being converted to M60A3s throughout Europe and the US. The M60A3 weighs 57.3 tons and carries a crew of four at a maximum road speed of 30 mph. Its cruising range is 280

Both pages: The M113 personnel carrier, workhorse of the cavalry and infantry for many years, will be replaced by the Bradley Fighting Vehicle in most units.

miles at 20 mph, and it is equipped with the 105mm M68 rifled cannon.

The Bradley Infantry Fighting Vehicle (IFV) provides the mechanized infantry with a full-track, lightly armored fighting vehicle. It carries a nine-man squad, including a commander, gunner, driver and six infantrymen who can fight dismounted or mounted, using the six firing port 5.66mm weapons, the 25mm automatic stabilized cannon mounted in the two-man turret, the 7.62mm machine gun and Tube Launched Optically Tracked Wire Guided (TOW) antitank guided missiles.

The Bradley Cavalry Fighting Vehicle (CFV) is used by the scout and armored cavalry units for screening, reconnaissance and security missions. The structure is identical to the Bradley IFV, except for the absence of firing-port weapons. The CFV carries a five-man crew for reconnaissance missions. Both Bradley vehicles provide day and night thermal-sight capability for the commander and gunner, and image-intensification night-vision capability for the driver.

The M113 Armored Personnel Carrier was designed to transport troops, equipment and cargo during combat operations. The current M113A2 is being replaced by the Bradley in infantry-squad-carrier and cavalry/scout functions. The M113 will continue to be upgraded for use as a mortar carrier, command post, MED-EVAC carrier and maintenance support vehicle beyond the year 2000. The M113A2 is made of aluminum and weighs 12.5 tons. It carries 11 men at a road speed of 42 mph and cross-country speed of 19 mph. It has an 11 hp engine and features a 50-caliber machine gun.

The AH-64 Apache, the Army's primary attack helicopter, is a fast-reacting airborne antitank weapon. In wartime, it would be dispatched to the heaviest enemy penetration and destroy, disrupt or delay the attackers

Left: **The Vulcan antiaircraft gun, mounted on a tank chassis.**

Below: **An AH-1S modernized Cobra attack helicopter in current configuration.**

long enough for friendly ground units and armor to arrive. Its two-man crew can navigate and attack in the darkness thanks to a Target Acquisition Designation Sight and Pilot Night Vision Sensor (TADS/PNVS). It is also equipped with a 30mm chain gun and 2.75-inch rockets. The Apache's mission weight is 14,660 lb and it can travel at 146 knots. The Apache, deployed in 1985, is supported in the field by the Cobra.

The AH-1S Cobra (the newer version of the AH-1, which was used extensively in Vietnam) is an attack helicopter with the primary mission of destroying light armored vehicles. However, its performance is limited, and it is now used as a complement to the Apache. The Cobra TOW missile system requires that the target be kept in crosshairs until impact, leaving it vulnerable to enemy missile and gunfire. Also, the Cobra is mostly limited to fair-weather performance. The Army has begun the Cobra Fleet Life Extension (FLEX) program, providing

Below: **A UH-60 Black Hawk transport helicopter hovers over marshland. The UH-60 is a highly effective tactical assault vehicle. The Black Hawk is also used for aeromedical evacuation.**

improvements to keep the Cobra in service for some time to come. The Cobra weighs 10,000 lb, flies at a speed of 129 knots, carries a crew of two and features eight TOW missiles, 2.75-inch rockets and a 20mm cannon. Its endurance is 2.2 to 2.9 hours. The Cobra is the attack version of the Huey utility helicopter; both aircraft have been in service with the Army for 20 years.

The M249 Squad Automatic Weapon

is a lightweight, one-man portable base of fire for infantry squads. In the 1970s, this role was filled by the M16A1 rifle, which was equipped with a bipod and fired in the automatic mode. The M249 is more stable, accurate and has a higher rate of fire than the M16A1.

Below: **A variant of the M113 personnel carrier, modified to carry the Vulcan antiaircraft gun, being loaded with blue practice rounds.**

AIR DEFENSE WEAPONS

Air defense weapons are ground-fire systems used to detect and engage enemy aircraft. They protect all ground-force elements, including troop formations, depots, lines of communication, air bases, key command and control facilities.

The Chaparral, the Army's short-range defense (SHORAD) surface-to-air missile system, provides protection for forward-deployed divisions and corps and for rear-theater areas. A self-propelled, self-contained system, it has excellent cross-country mobility. The launch station is also self-contained and can be taken off the carrier and used from the ground. It is supersonic and lightweight, and has fire-and-forget capability as well as an infrared homing guidance system that can engage both approaching and receding targets. Its targets are visually acquired, which has posed a problem at night and in bad weather, but the addition of Forward-Looking Infrared (FLIR) night sight has improved visibility. Chaparral has an Identification Friend-or-Foe (IFF) subsystem, which helps the gunner identify friendly targets. It carries four ready missiles on launch rails and an additional eight missiles in storage.

The Army had high hopes for the Sgt York Division Air Defense (DIVAD) gun system as an eventual replacement for the Chaparral and the Vulcan in close-range, low-altitude air defense. However, it was canceled in production by Secretary of Defense Caspar Weinberger on 27 August 1985. Weinberger stated that the weapon's performance did not warrant the additional 3 billion dollars necessary to complete a project on which the Pentagon had already spent 1.8 billion dollars since 1978. The Sgt York (named after World War I hero Alvin C York) was designed as a mobile, radar-controlled, all-weather gun to provide air-defense coverage for maneuver troops against Soviet ground-attack aircraft and antitank guided-missile-launching helicopters. Extensive field testing in 1984 showed that the computerized aim of the Sgt York was not much better than the systems it was

Opposite above: **The Chaparral, a short-ranged air-defense missile system.**

Opposite below: **The ill-fated Sgt York air defense system, scrapped in 1985 for being over budget and under qualified.**

designed to replace and that it was quite vulnerable to attack by enemy aircraft. Each component of the system worked well separately — but not together — and the computer that coordinated the system tended to malfunction. Despite the critics' assertions that the weapon was too complex and expensive, the Army wanted to continue the project, believing that the technical problems could be worked out and that solving those current problems was preferable to waiting years for a new-generation antiaircraft gun to be delivered.

The Stinger, a shoulder-fired, heat-seeking, infrared homing-missile system, provides air defense to even the smallest units. It is designed to withstand the rigors of the battlefield and requires no maintenance in the field.

The Patriot is the Army's new, all-altitude missile system. It has fast-reac-

Above: **A soldier aims the Stinger, a 35 lb, shoulder-fired, man-portable guided-missile system that provides air defense against low-level aircraft.**

tion capability, high firepower and the ability to operate in a severe electronic-countermeasure environment. It requires less equipment, less operational manpower and fewer repair parts than the Hawk, the low- to-medium-altitude missile system that the Patriot was designed to replace.

FIRE SUPPORT SYSTEMS

Fire support systems generate indirect firepower. They include cannons, rockets, missiles, and target acquisition and communication systems.

The Multiple Launch Rocket System (MLRS) is a free-flight, area-fire, artillery rocket system with the

This page: The Multiple Launch Rocket System (MLRS), designed to complement cannon artillery in combat, can operate day and night in all types of weather. Its surface-to-surface free rockets have a range in excess of 30 kilometers, and a 12-rocket load can cover an area the size of up to six football fields.

Above and below: The Multiple Launch Rocket System (MLRS). The MLRS carries a crew of three that controls the system, whether the on-board fire control computer is on automatic or manual. The tracked mobile launcher has cross-country capability comparable to the M1 tank and can be part of a combined-arms, tank-led combat team.

primary mission of counterfire and suppression of enemy air defenses. It supplements cannon artillery fires by delivering large volumes of fire in short time spans. It was fielded in 1983.

The Army employs three howitzer cannons: the M109A2 and M110A2 self-propelled cannons and the M198 medium towed cannon. All are capable of launching a variety of nuclear and nonnuclear munitions.

The Battery Computer System (BCS) works in conjunction with the howitzers to provide improved fire control. The system consists of a computer terminal at the field artillery battery headquarters and a display unit at each weapon. The BCS receives firing-data requests, computes the data and sends it to each howitzer. The BCS can also be used with the MLRS.

COMBAT SUPPORT SYSTEMS

Combat support systems provide operational assistance to the combat arms. They include engineer support systems, which are used in combat engineer efforts and mine/countermine warfare, and theater tactical intelligence systems, which provide theater/tactical commanders with information to support planning, the readiness of forces for combat, and the conduct of combat operations.

COMBAT-SERVICE SUPPORT SYSTEMS

Combat-service support systems provide tactical units with maintenance, supply, medical, transportation and other vital services. They range from commercially available, four-wheel-drive trucks adapted for Army use to utility helicopters. Some primary weapons from this group are discussed below.

The Black Hawk UH-60A utility helicopter is used in air assault, air cavalry and aeromedical evacuation missions. It adds considerably to the Army's division mobility. In a single lift, it can reposition an 11-man fully equipped squad or a 105mm howitzer, its crew of six, and up to 30 rounds of ammunition. It is more easily maintained in the field than any other helicopter. It travels at 145 knots with

Opposite: **The crew of a UH-60 Black Hawk about to settle the big bird on a golden-brown field. The Black Hawk's missions include combat service support.**

an endurance of 2.3 hours and features two 7.62mm machine guns. The Black Hawk was first fielded in high-priority units in the continental US and Korea in 1984, and to WESTCOM and FORSCOM in 1985. During Operation Urgent Fury in Grenada, a Black Hawk reportedly took 45 rounds of groundfire and kept flying.

The CH-47 Chinook, the Army's medium-lift helicopter, is used to move ammunition, repair parts, petroleum, artillery, troops and special weapons. It has undergone major modernization programs since first being fielded in 1962. CH-47A, B and C models are being upgraded to the D model, which will expand the life of the fleet past the year 2000. The Chinook weighs 50,000 lb, travels at 158 knots and is capable of carrying 33 troops. Its maximum cargo load is 24,000 lb.

TACTICAL COMMAND, CONTROL AND COMMUNICATION SYSTEMS

The Tactical Command, Control and Communications C^3 systems allow a commander to locate and communicate with his tactical unit, even in an area with enemy electronic countermeasures. They range from a single channel ground and airborne radio system to the Defense Satellite Communications System (DSCS) for which the Army develops and fields satellite earth terminals for all the armed forces.

Above and below: **The CH-47 Chinook medium-lift helicopter carrying an external load, and a string of UH-60 Black Hawks on desert maneuvers.**

NEW TECHNOLOGIES

In order to be prepared for the 1990s and beyond, the Army is developing new 'leverage' technologies that may completely change the ways in which wars are fought. The Army's new thrusts in technology include dramatic improvements in battlefield information communications; self-contained munition technologies that will allow munitions to independently seek and home in on hostile targets; and biotechnology, which promises to improve the prevention and treatment of casualties and diseases through rapid identification, new vaccines and detection of chemical and biological agents. Enhanced hands-on training programs will improve operators' performance in the use of sophisticated equipment. These programs will underlie all new technology thrusts as well as ongoing engineering developments and product improvements.

The AH-64 Apache attack helicopter, silhouetted against a stunning sunset. Army helicopters are named after American Indian tribes.

TRAINING AND EDUCATION THE GOOD GET BETTER

The emphasis on state-of-the-art weapons does not overshadow the importance of the soldier; without a competent human to run it, the most sophisticated system is little more than a hunk of hardware. The benefits of a weapon are lost if the soldier doesn't completely understand it and the strategies involved in using it. A major challenge for the Army is to integrate new equipment with well-trained, intelligent, capable, combat-ready personnel.

The Training and Doctrine Command (TRADOC) has the complex and vital job of ensuring that soldiers are ready to fight and win whenever and wherever they are needed. TRADOC decides how the Army will fight as well as how it will be equipped and organized. TRADOC conducts training at 17 installations, 15 branch schools, 8 specialist schools, 3 integrating centers, over 1000 ROTC programs and the Command and General Staff College. Its 1984 training budget was 5 billion dollars. A variety of training programs is used to develop and maintain quality soldiers and officers. They range from Initial Entry Training to computer-simulated and live-com-

bat exercises. Initial Entry Training consists of Basic Training, Advanced Individual Training (AIT) and One Station Unit Training. Soldiers who will serve in noncombat arms receive Basic Training followed by Advanced Individual Training in their military occupational specialties, which may range from administration and finance to missile repair. Soldiers entering combat arms branches such as infantry, artillery, and armor receive One Station Unit Training, which combines basic and specialized training. Women are trained at five out of the eight Army training centers. Since by law they may not serve in combat arms or direct combat support, they continue on to AIT. Throughout his or her term of service, a soldier may be eligible for continued specialty training.

BASIC TRAINING

Basic Training transforms a civilian into a soldier in eight weeks. Soldiers are trained at platoon level, providing the opportunity for individual attention. The standard is excellence, not adequacy. Basic is divided into three phases. The first phase (two

Opposite: **Recruits stand at attention before their drill sergeant. The drill sergeant is responsible for the recruits' health and welfare during basic training.**

Left: **Prior to actual basic training, recruits spend a few days at a reception station, where the men receive a close shave and all are issued Army gear.**

weeks) covers basic soldier skills, from drill training to M16A2 rifle instruction and nuclear, biological and chemical warfare defense. The second phase (three weeks) includes weapons training and map reading; basic skills are reinforced and developed. In the last three weeks, tactical training, field training and the physical endurance confidence course are mastered. Emphasis is on teamwork and attitude. When the civilian has successfully become the soldier, he or she moves on to more advanced training in a particular Army occupation.

OFFICER TRAINING

Several paths can be followed by the man or woman who wishes to be an Army officer:

- Reserve Officers Training Corps (ROTC)
- The United States Military Academy at West Point
- Officer Candidate School
- Direct commission (civilian with special skill)

ROTC is the largest source of officers for the Army, providing about 70 percent of the Army's officers annually. ROTC students join the program while attending college. After graduating and being accepted for duty, he or she enters Officer Basic Course (OBC), which prepares lieutenants for duty in active and reserve units. They are taught to lead, train and fight, and are qualified for branch duties. The 20-week Officer Advanced Course (OAC) prepares the officer for unit command in his or her future branch. Combat leaders learn to move, shoot and communicate; combat support leaders learn to lead support troops. For example, OAC students at the armor school in Fort Knox concentrate on tank-company command, tactics and combined arms doctrine. The signal school teaches electronics, computers and tactical communications devices. All OACs include hands-on tactical training in preparation for leading soldiers in combat.

Since it was founded in 1802, the United States Military Academy at

From top: **The path of potential soldiers. A young man at the crossroads; Army recruits are sworn in; and, any recruit's final destination, Basic Training. The recruit at left is discovering that the discipline begins before he's even off the bus. He has eight more rigorous weeks ahead.**

Above: A drill sergeant offers a word of advice to a recruit at Fort Campbell, Kentucky. Many soldiers remember their 'DI' with respect, if not fondness. Anyway, they remember him.

Below: Recruits on the march. From basic training to computer-simulated battle and overseas force deployment exercises, the Army provides tough, realistic training.

Below: Mud-caked but jubilant infantrymen of the 2nd Infantry Training Brigade, Fort Benning, Georgia after completion of a confidence course. These soldiers are undergoing One Station Unit Training, in which the unit stays together through basic and advanced training. The recruit giving the 'thumbs up' sign *(left)* can be seen battling the course in the inset *(opposite below).*

An aerial view of the United States Military Academy at West Point, looking north up the Hudson River. West Point is the site of the oldest continuously occupied military post in the country. Its strategic location in a narrow 'S' turn on the Hudson made it ideal for General George Washington's headquarters in 1779.

Above: **The US Military Academy's Battle Monument at Trophy Point.**

Opposite: **The Cadet Chapel of West Point after a picturesque snowfall.**

West Point has produced a long line of distinguished alumni including Ulysses S Grant, Douglas MacArthur, Dwight D Eisenhower and astronaut Edwin 'Buzz' Aldrin. Today, West Point graduates about 900 officers a year, providing excellent academic training as well as military training. Preparation for a military career includes field and classroom instruction in military skills, an intensive physical education program and practical and classroom training in leadership. During the academic year, military instruction is limited to two hours per week of theory and classroom work; however, the summer months are devoted to practical, in-the-field military training. After completing the four-year program, the cadet enters service with the Army as a second lieutenant and is trained by the branch to which he or she is assigned.

The Army's Officer Candidate School trains enlisted men who are college

Above and overleaf: **Cadets march in front of Washington Hall; hats fill the air as West Point cadets celebrate their graduation with the traditional signal.**

graduates or obtaining a degree. They receive 22 weeks of training before advancing to OCS and OAC.

Certain professionals may be offered a direct commission as an Army officer. Doctors, nurses, lawyers and chaplains are in demand and may receive commissions based on their training.

Other training opportunities are available to officers after they have spent time as commanders or staff officers. The Combined Arms and Services Staff School offers an intensive course that emphasizes staff skills for a variety of missions in combat, combat support and combat-service support units. The Command and General Staff College prepares field grade officers for the responsibilities of command and staff.

Portraits of women in the Army: A drill sergeant advises a recruit during basic *(left)*; a recruit combats an obstacle course *(top)*; a Military Police officer communicates by walkie-talkie *(middle)*; a paratrooper after completing her jump *(bottom)*. Women are an integral part of the Army, filling ranks from private to general. Career opportunities are available to women in all occupational specialties not directly combat related. A small percentage of women, who will be involved in support services, are eligible for airborne training.

Above: **US Army Rangers prepare to be airlifted to a remote area for maneuvers.**

Left: **A wooden tower is used to simulate rappelling out of helicopters.**

COMBAT TRAINING

The lack of realistic combat training prior to actual combat has cost many lives throughout the Army's history. Today, various types of combat training exercises — from simulations to the full deployment of units overseas — are used to test and improve combat readiness.

The Army participates in many large-scale exercises throughout the world: 'Reforger' is an operational maneuver and training exercise that takes place in Germany. US-based active and reserve forces deploy to Europe, where they train in what could be their wartime environment. Similarly, Third Army deploys to Egypt for 'Bright Star' exercises every other year.

The National Training Center (NTC) at Fort Irwin, California is unique among training centers. Its size and scope allow for the training of task-force battalions whose weaponry has grown beyond the limits of other centers in the nation. NTC offers a vast

Above: **A smiling 'wounded' soldier is evacuated during training exercises.**

Right: **A drill sergeant instructs a recruit on the M16 rifle range.**

maneuver space, well-trained opposing forces (OPFOR), live fire, an instrumented battlefield and standardized, computerized evaluation. Perhaps the NTC's most unique feature is the OPFOR, who are dressed in Soviet uniforms and whose weapons are modified to look like Soviet weapons.

Since space and live munitions are not always available to meet the expanding training requirements, battle simulators are seen as an economical yet highly effective alternative to 'live' training. The Army training battle-simulation system (ARTBASS) is an automated, interactive system for maneuver battalion commanders and their staffs. By 1987, the aviation combined-arms team training (ACATT) computer simulator will provide total, combined training to the scout, attack team and battle captain while saving fuel, ammunition and hours. The use of computerized battle simulators is increasing as systems become more sophisticated, and they will be heavily relied upon in the future.

A soldier is schooled in the use of aerial photos during a field training exercise. Maneuvers are intended to be as close as possible to the real thing.

Above: Mechanized infantrymen run alongside a Bradley Fighting Vehicle during an exercise at the Infantry Training Center at Fort Benning.

Below: Combat training involves high tech, such as the position location reporting system *(left)*, and old-fashioned crawling under barbed wire *(right)*.

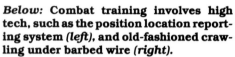

Below: Rangers man a mortar position during field maneuvers. The number of Rangers has increased recently as the Army restructures itself to meet the ever-changing threats it faces.

Opposite: Trainees engaged in hand-to-hand combat. The soldier of today is better trained than ever before in basic combat skills, as well as in the evolving concepts of modern warfare.

Above and opposite: Portraits of 'Border Star 85.' A member of the 9th Infantry Division, which demonstrated a frontal assault at the Donna-Anna range north of El Paso, Texas *(above)*; and Pvt Darren Rollinson, M60 tank crew member.

Above: Comprehensive training in nuclear, biological and chemical warfare defense is vital to every soldier's safety.

Below: A soldier in a tight spot during Ranger training.

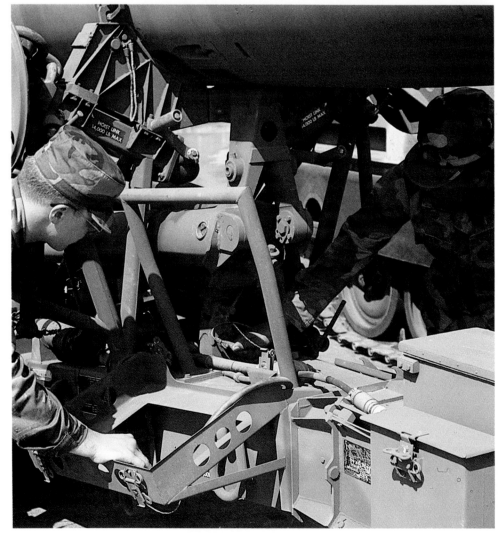

Numerous types of training programs are available to Army personnel. Soldiers and officers alike may spend time cracking a book *(above)*; or receiving hands-on technical training, such as that offered at the Redstone Arsenal in Alabama *(left)*. Academic and technical training not only further military careers, but promise broader civilian employment opportunities.

EDUCATION

The Army sets high standards for its people; then it helps them to achieve these standards. Today's soldier should not only be combat-ready, but knowledgeable and highly motivated. The Army Continuing Education System (ACES) helps soldiers and officers to improve their skills, and therefore their success in and out of the Army, with many levels of programs — from basic reading to doctoral degrees.

Unfortunately, some soldiers do not possess the basic reading, writing and mathematical skills necessary to advance in the Army. Basic skills are taught to these soldiers, and those who do not have a high school diploma are strongly urged to acquire one by taking the high school equivalency test or enrolling in classes offered on their bases.

Top and above: SFC Curtis explains the intricacies of the land combat support system to Pvt Blowe at Redstone Arsenal, Alabama; a soldier fine tunes television equipment in an Army TV studio.

Above and above right: A soldier at work at her computer terminal; and learning the fine points of operating a radar scope. Much of the Army's technical training is transferable to civilian careers. The Army's

training and education programs promise that the good get better, and women can and do fill critical positions in all components except active combat which is not allowed by law.

Throughout their careers, all soldiers and officers are encouraged to further their education. Officers are now required to have a bachelor's degree, and an officer is not usually able to achieve the rank of major without a master's degree. The Army pays a percentage of tuition (up to 90 percent) at civilian schools, depending on rank and length of service. High school, college and graduate courses can be taken through the mail by personnel unable to attend classes for reasons of logistics or scheduling.

Each Army base has an education center that assists personnel in achiev-

ing their education goals. Material and facilities are provided so that soldiers can work alone or in a group to increase their knowledge in their Military Occupational Specialty (MOS). Military correspondence courses are available as well. Education centers help in preparation for the Skill Qualification Test (SQT) taken annually by most enlisted personnel. SQT results figure heavily in promotion and re-enlistment considerations. In fact, a low score on the SQT, followed by no improvement, can result in a discharge from the Army. In 1984, 25 percent of Army personnel allowed to re-enlist

would not have met the re-enlistment standards without assistance from the education and training programs.

The Army teaches vocational-technical skills, such as computer programming or auto mechanics, for on-the-job or personal use. An apprenticeship program documents work in specific jobs for use in obtaining civilian employment if and when a soldier leaves the Army.

With the educational opportunities afforded today's soldiers and officers, it is not suprising that in a recent survey the major reason for joining the Army was 'to get a good education.'

THE UNITED STATES ARMY IN ACTION

Two recent military involvements illustrate both the effectiveness of the Army's light forces and the need for improved capability to engage in low-level conflict.

Light, flexible and highly mobile troops were used with great success during Operation Urgent Fury in Grenada; conditions in Central America show the advantage of structuring troops to handle low-intensity conflict effectively. To this end, special forces and Ranger units are being expanded and more light infantry troops organized to deal with this continuing threat.

GRENADA

On 25 October 1983, President Ronald Reagan ordered US Army and Marine forces to the tiny Caribbean island of Grenada to rescue nearly 1000 Americans thought to be in danger in the wake of a bloody Communist coup. Marxist Prime Minister Maurice Bishop had been murdered by members of the 'Revolutionary Military Council' led by General Hudson

Opposite: **A member of the 101st Airborne ('Screaming Eagles') studies a map during 'Bright Star' exercises in Egypt.**

Right: **Infantrymen use camouflage gear and natural foliage for cover in combat.**

Austin, and the nation was in chaos. The US military operation, called Urgent Fury, had an urgent mission: prevent a repeat of the 1980 Iran hostage situation.

Grenada had been a British possession until 1974, and in 1979 Bishop overthrew the newly formed government and established relations with Cuba. US intelligence reports of Soviet and Cuban military projects, including military training areas, storage facilities for ammunition and supplies as well as a runway capable of accommodating Soviet long-range offensive aircraft were released in March 1983. In October, the military council, which controlled Grenada's 2000-man army, had closed schools and nonessential businesses and set a four-day, twenty-four-hour 'shoot on sight' curfew.

Near dawn on 25 October, US Army Rangers from the 1st and 2nd battalions of the 75th Infantry parachuted onto the Point Salines Cuban-built airfield, located on the southern tip of the island and surrounded by water on three sides, at some points as close as 35 feet. With no reserve parachutes, the Rangers jumped in at 500 feet to better avoid hostile gunfire. Amid unexpectedly heavy antiaircraft fire, the first two US Air Force C-130 transports were forced to abort their approaches.

Above and left: **The 82nd Airborne played a large part in the Grenada rescue/invasion in 1983. After securing Salines Airport on Grenada, they moved out on patrol** *(above).*

The third aircraft sneaked in during a short lull and dumped about 50 Rangers onto the 10,000-foot runway. They alone fought Cuban and Granadian forces for 20 minutes, as a resurgence of antiaircraft fire kept the last four C-130s from closing in. The stranded Rangers quickly radioed nearby AC-130 Spectre gunships, which suppressed enemy fire long enough to allow the rest of the Rangers to jump.

After landing, the Rangers — still

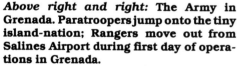

Above right and right: **The Army in Grenada. Paratroopers jump onto the tiny island-nation; Rangers move out from Salines Airport during first day of operations in Grenada.**

under fire — cleared the runway of barbed-wire barricades, rollers, trucks and bulldozers, while the 1st battalion secured the northeast end of the airstrip where the enemy had established positions in building foundations and houses. Within approximately two hours, the Rangers had secured the airport, enabling US Air Force C-141s carrying two battalions of the 82nd Airborne Division to land. Meanwhile, Marines of the I-84 Amphibious Group had secured Pearls

Airport, a commercial airstrip at the northern end of the island.

At dawn the next day, 82nd Airborne troops attacked a compound of 10 to 15 concrete buildings in the hills one mile north of the airstrip. They were met with heavy sniper fire, which they returned with M-203 HE rounds. Failing to locate the source of enemy fire, they called in Navy A-7 Corsairs to strafe the compound area. The defenders surrendered, but not before several US soldiers were wounded.

Heavy casualties were prevented at one point in the rescue/invasion by a quick-thinking soldier. His unit was trapped in a house surrounded by Cuban forces; using his AT&T long-distance credit card, he telephoned Army officers in Fort Bragg, North Carolina and informed them of the

Opposite: **82d Airborne troops prepare to move out from the Salines Airport.**

Below: **UH-60 Black Hawks damaged during Operation Urgent Fury on Grenada. Three were disabled on 27 October.**

unit's dangerous position. Fort Bragg contacted the Air Force, which sent in AC-130 Spectre gunships to disperse the Cubans and relieve the unit.

Also on 26 October, Army and Marine forces combined in a heliborne assault on the Grand Anse campus of St George's Medical College, rescuing over 200 students. One student provided the world with on-the-spot action reports via his ham radio for more than 30 hours, relaying accounts of students rolling under beds and diving into bathtubs to avoid stray bullets. The following day, more than 200 additional students were rescued on the Lance aux Epines peninsula. Although some students later insisted that they were in no danger, most expressed gratitude to the US forces for their courageous undertaking.

Hostilities officially ceased on 2 November, but more than 2000 US troops still remained to clear out snipers and hidden Communist-made weapons. By December a few hundred US troops remained in Grenada in an

advisory capacity. In all, 18 US troops were killed and 116 were wounded.

HONDURAS

The presence of US troops in Honduras has been a subject of heated debate since the first group of Green Berets arrived in March of 1982 to train Honduran soldiers guarding their border with El Salvador. In 1980, the US had begun military aid to the government of El Salvador in the form of 35 million dollars and 20 Green Berets as military advisers in El Salvador's struggle against revolutionary guerilla troops. The US felt it had the evidence to support its claim that the troubled country was in danger of becoming a Soviet satellite.

Fearing involvement in another Vietnam-type conflict, many members of Congress and US citizens have objected strongly to US military presence in Central America. Nevertheless, it continues, and the Army plays a large

role in that presence in Honduras. In 1985, about 1200 Army personnel were on temporary duty in Honduras as part of Joint Task Force Bravo, the headquarters and support element for the joint US-Honduran training exercises that take place regularly in that country. Joint Task Force Bravo is headquartered at the Honduran air base at Palmerola; there are six or seven additional bases and small airstrips in Honduras that are also used by US troops.

Ongoing training exercises range greatly in size, emphasis and dura-tion. The 'Big Pine' exercises have involved as many as two thousand US soldiers at one time. A recent road-building exercise, 'Cabana 85,' lasted three months and involved mostly engineer troops. 'Big Pine III' brought US tanks to Honduras for the first time. Some counterinsurgency training lasts only a few days and involves fewer than 100 troops. Army forces, aside from the support troops, include special forces and active and reserve combat units that are deployed to Honduras to train and be trained.

The Defense Department gives three reasons for the US presence in Honduras. To demonstrate US resolve in Central America and to improve Honduras' capacity for self-defense, while providing a place for US troops to train for low-level conflict. The Army will be in Honduras in this capacity as long as the US-Honduran agreement benefits both countries.

Previous page: **MPs listen for intruders during maneuvers.**

Above: **A paratroop drop during training exercises in Honduras, and a soldier gives the thumbs up sign to a driver.**

Below: An Army truck is guided aboard an Air Force C-5 Galaxy in Honduras. The Army plays an integral part of the controversial presence of US troops in Honduras.

Below: Honduran troops board a US Air Force C-130 transport plane for deployment to their training site. US-Honduran training maneuvers are commonplace in Honduras.

Previous page: **Camouflaged infantrymen aim their M16s. Infantry training includes individual and squad tactical maneuvers as well as patrolling.**

THE UNITED STATES ARMY TODAY

In 1775 the Continental Army, though outnumbered, beat the British because it adapted to its environment and maximized its resources. Today, this spirit is reflected in the Army's major restructuring program undertaken since the early 1970s. Adaptability is the keynote in these programs. The Army must be ready to move into any terrain with a hard-hitting combat force.

To ensure combat readiness, the Army is improving training methods, modernizing weapons and recruiting personnel capable of utilizing state-of-the-art technology and constantly evolving strategy. Units are being redesigned to allow the rapid deployment necessary to meet the ever-expanding spectrum of threats. This modernization has been extended to the Army Reserves and National Guard as the Army maximizes its present resources. A smaller, more flexible Army is in keeping with the principles of the AirLand Battle Doctrine.

This evolving doctrine and the program it established will ensure that the Army will remain a dynamic force throughout the world.

Top left: **Soldiers await a call from their unit in their jeep, which has been converted with tape and burlap to reduce reflection and avoid detection.**

Top right: **Soldiers practice moving and shooting in cumbersome gas masks.**

Right: **Reserve troops undergo exacting nuclear, biological and chemical warfare defense training.**

Far right and overleaf: **Army Reserve infantrymen on tactical maneuvers.**

INDEX

Below: **A soldier guards an Air Force C-5A Galaxy transport plane.**

Overleaf: **The Golden Knights, the Army's parachute demonstration team.**